$\mathcal{B}$EAUTY
Basics

Quick *and*
Easy Tips *for*
Hair, Skin, *and*
Makeup

PETER LAMAS

Strength
& Honor

BRONZE
BOW PUB.

The information in this book is for educational purposes only and is not recommended as a means of diagnosing or treating an illness. Neither the publisher nor author is engaged in rendering professional advice or services to the individual reader. All matters regarding physical and mental health should be supervised by a health practitioner knowledgeable in treating that particular condition. Neither the author nor the publisher shall be liable or responsible for any loss, injury, or damage allegedly arising from any information or suggestion in this book.

Beauty Basics
Copyright © 2003 Peter Lamas
All Scripture quotations, unless otherwise indicated, are taken from the Holy Bible, New International Version®. NIV®. Copyright © 1973, 1978, 1984 by International Bible Society. Used by permission of Zondervan Publishing House. All rights reserved.
ISBN 1-932458-07-7
Published by Bronze Bow Publishing, Inc.,
2600 East 26th Street, Minneapolis, MN 55406.
You can reach us on the Internet at
WWW.BRONZEBOWPUBLISHING.COM
Literary development and cover/interior design by
Koechel Peterson & Associates, Inc., Minneapolis, Minnesota.
Manufactured in the United States of America

CONTENTS

CHAPTER ONE
BEAUTY TIPS . . . OR MYTHS 7

CHAPTER TWO
LAYING THE RIGHT FOUNDATION 11

CHAPTER THREE
BLUSH AND CONTOURING TECHNIQUES 22

CHAPTER FOUR
CREATING BEAUTIFUL EYEBROWS 30

CHAPTER FIVE
THE ART OF CUSTOM EYES 36

CHAPTER SIX
LASHES 101 42

CHAPTER SEVEN
GREAT LOOKING LIPS 47

CHAPTER EIGHT
SKIN-CARE TIPS 52

CHAPTER NINE
TIPS ON HAIR 56

BOOKS BY PETER LAMAS

Beauty & Health Glossary
Beauty Basics
Dying to Be Beautiful
The Truth About Sun Exposure
Ultimate Anti-Aging Secrets

ABOUT THE AUTHOR

PETER LAMAS is Founder and Chairman of Lamas Beauty International, one of the fastest growing and respected natural beauty products manufacturers in the United States. He has been a major force in the beauty industry for more than 30 years. Peter's career began in New York City as an apprentice to trailblazers Vidal Sassoon and Paul Mitchell, providing the opportunity to work with some of the most famous and beautiful women of our time. His expertise in the areas of hair care, skin care, and makeup has given him a client list that reads like a *who's who of celebrities*.

His work has spanned numerous films, television, video, and print projects, including designing the gorgeous makeup used on the set of the epic film, *Titanic*. Peter has worked with the great names in fashion and beauty photography, including Richard Avedon, Irving Penn, and Francesco Scavullo. His work has been seen in photo shoots in leading magazines, such as *Vogue, Harper's Bazaar, Glamour,* and *Mademoiselle*.

Peter regularly appears on television and in the media in North and South America, Europe, and Asia. He travels extensively across the globe, speaking to women of many different cultures about how they can realize their potential to be beautiful both inside and out, especially educating them about the facts and myths on beauty products.

Cuban born Peter Lamas immigrated to New York in 1961. Several years later, while pursuing a career as a commercial artist, Peter decided to finance his education by doing hair and makeup. As a result, he discovered he not only had a flair for doing hair and makeup, but he truly enjoyed helping each client look her best.

Peter's life has been dedicated to helping women feel good about themselves, by helping them realize their vast potential for personal beauty. To him, beauty is not just about the perfect haircut or makeup; it's about the full package. He can make just about any woman look absolutely stunning; but if she doesn't feel beautiful, she won't be. Beauty is very personal, and contrary to the cliché "that beauty is in the eye of the beholder," he came to realize that it is also in the eye of the possessor, because what makes us truly attractive to others is the projection of our self-esteem. Grace, confidence, and personality play a major role in attractiveness.

Peter's web site, www.lamasbeauty.com, is one of the largest women's beauty and health information resources on the Internet, through which he and a host of contributing writers keep women and men informed on important beauty and health topics.

Mr. Lamas is an innovative product developer in the cosmetics industry and recently received the distinguished honor from *Health Magazine* for developing the "Best Moisturizer of the Year." You can learn more about Peter's company, Lamas Beauty International, by visiting www.lamasbeauty.com or emailing him directly at peterlamas@lamasbeauty.com.

CHAPTER ONE

Beauty Tips . . .
OR MYTHS?

"The Lord does not look at the things man looks at. Man looks at the outward appearance, but the Lord looks at the heart."
—1 SAMEUL 16:7

HAVING worked in the "world of beauty" for the last 30 years, I am excited to place in your hands the practical tips and beauty wisdom I have learned. Some tips are timeless classics that will help you highlight your natural beauty. Others can help you create the next look-of-the-moment. Together, you'll find just what you need to achieve a sleek, professional look—fast and easy—right at home.

Some beauty tips are handed down from generation to generation and are excellent. But many of them are pure mythology, so hold your beauty tips with a light hand as you may find they simply are not true. Here's a few myths I've heard over and over again, which should be dismissed forever.

1. *Drink eight glasses of water daily* to hydrate your skin. Drinking water is essential for your body's health—inside. However, your skin becomes dry from external aggressors—cold, sun, wind, pollution, even room heaters and air conditioners—so it needs something that works from the outside in, as in a moisturizer. My suggestion is that right after you wash your face or shower, massage in your moisturizer while the skin is still damp to get the benefits of the water and the moisturizer.

2. *Smoking and caffeine cause dry skin.* Tests show that caffeine has no direct effect on your skin, but it does deplete water from the body. Smoking only works indirectly to age your skin, by decreasing blood circulation so the skin doesn't get as much oxygen—which is essential in creating and maintaining healthy skin cells. In addition, the repetitive eye squinting and pursing of the lips while you smoke can cause premature wrinkling around the eyes and the mouth.

3. *Baby oil or petroleum jelly heals dry, chapped skin better than moisturizer.* Baby oil and petroleum jelly can act as barriers to help prevent further moisture loss, but they don't put anything back in the bank. In fact, they can clog pores, causing havoc on your skin. Moisturize dry, chapped areas with a rich, hydrating moisturizer.

4. *You can scrub acne away.* Coarse, heavy-grained exfoliators are often recommended for acne-prone, oily skin. But used too often and too vigorously, they can actually aggravate acne by opening the cysts and encouraging the skin to produce even more oil to compensate for what's being ruthlessly stripped away. Instead, use a medium-strength exfoliator suspended in a gel or paste, and don't overdo it.

One word about beauty before I begin with my tips. In my upcoming book, *BeautyWalk,* I devote an entire chapter to the theme of beauty. I believe that God made you beautiful just the way you are! Women need to embrace that wondrous truth, and understand that who they are is perfect. Real beauty comes from within, not by trying to force yourself into today's cultural definition of beauty (which is an absurd and always changing ideal). To allow beauty to be defined outside of yourself is to chase an elusive dream.

My advice to you is: "Do what suits you best. You

can't force your body to be what it isn't." It is unnecessary to try to create an illusion of what your body isn't meant to be. Your body size or look does not define who you are or give or take away your self-worth. Self-esteem is not a function of dress size or facial structure. Genuine self-worth exists with the inner peace and acceptance of the person living inside your beautiful body.

I offer my beauty tips because I know that when you feel good about yourself by enhancing your natural looks, you'll find more joy in your life.

CHAPTER TWO

Laying the Right FOUNDATION

Ever wonder how today's models and movie stars achieve their beautiful, seemingly flawless faces? They know one of the best kept secrets to "creating" beauty: Build from the ground up. In the world of makeup and "face design," that means choosing the right foundation and perfecting your application technique.

The importance of foundation cannot be underestimated. It's the unsung hero of makeup—the simple backdrop that creates "tone," hides imperfections, and brings together all the other makeup "elements."

There are two basic steps to choosing the right foundation—determining which type of foundation is right for your skin type and then choosing the right color.

FIVE TYPES OF FOUNDATION

Choosing the right type of foundation has a lot to do with a person's skin type—dry, oily, or normal—and a little to do with preference. The following guidelines will help you choose the type that's right for you.

Liquid foundations are the most versatile type of foundation, suitable for a full range of skin types. They blend easily, are available in varying degrees of coverage, and often feature moisturizers in their dry-skin versions. Most liquid foundations are water-based, although some are oil-based.

Cream foundations are known for their heavier coverage and more intense moisturizing properties, making them ideal for normal, dry, and especially extra-dry skin. A word of caution, however: They're often oil-based and should be avoided by those with a tendency toward breakouts.

Compact foundations are ideal for on-the-go women who can't be bothered with cumbersome bottles and jars. Especially suitable for oily and normal skin types, compact foundations deliver a light sheer matte coverage when applied with a dry sponge, and a heavier matte coverage when applied with a wet sponge.

Stick foundations seem wonderfully reminiscent of crayons—just "color" in your face and you're ready to go!—but unfortunately, application isn't quite so simple. Although stick foundations, which are best suited for normal skin, offer the convenience of a built-in concealer, their heavier texture requires skillful blending with a moistened sponge.

Tinted moisturizer foundations offer the lightest coverage available, delivering a sheer healthy glow to the wearer. Similar to liquid foundations, they're ideal for a full range of skin types. Their moisturizing properties help protect against the dry skin that comes from overexposure to the wind, sun, and other outdoor elements, and as an added bonus, they often come with SPF protection.

DEWY OR MATTE?

One of the most common makeup questions is whether to use a dewy or matte type of foundation finish. Although these two finishes are often positioned as "fashion" statements, the simple truth is that each is most suitable for various types of skin.

While matte finishes are ideal for all types of skin, they are especially suited for oilier skin, because they help counteract and control the oil that causes undesirable sheen and shine. One possible exception is during the winter months, when the air is often dryer and oiliness is less of a problem.

The use of dewy finishes should be limited mostly to non-oily skin types, which are not as susceptible to sheen and shine.

Acne-prone skin types should avoid compact foundation because the sponge grabs bacteria, which breeds in the closed dark space. Sheer foundation is best on blemished, freckle-lined skin, as a heavy base foundation will accentuate pimples and wrinkles.

THE "COLOR" OF PERFECT FOUNDATION

Once you've determined the right type of foundation for your skin type, you're ready to choose the right color or tone. This is an area where a lot of women make one of their biggest beauty mistakes. Fortunately, it doesn't have to be that way. There are several secrets to choosing wisely.

The Disappearing Act. It's important to remember that foundation is a "backdrop" to your makeup. It's meant to create the kind of "perfect" skin we see in all the fashion magazines. Its role is to blend away blemishes and create an even, flawless skin tone. It should do its job and simply "disappear" from sight. Perfect foundation should be indistinguishable from perfect skin.

Color Me Natural. Foundation can only be perfect if it mimics the skin's natural tone, which leads us to one of the most common mistakes made when choosing a foundation color: Choosing something other than a yellow-based tone, which is the only tone that's found in human skin. Although makeup companies are only too happy to sell foundations that feature pink, peach, and orange tones, such products should be strictly avoided. For a perfect start to a beautiful face, only a yellow-based foundation will do.

Seeing Clearly. In order to choose the perfect tone of foundation, it's necessary to view the tone in natural lighting. If you're applying the foundation in a department store, it's often possible to take a mirror over to a windowed area or an entryway to see if it matches your skin tone and "disappears" from sight. Fluorescent and other types of artificial lighting can distort the way a color actually looks.

Taking the Test. There's only one way to see if a color is actually the right one for your skin tone, and that's to put it on. The secret is to choose a color that most closely matches your neck and then swipe a little of the foundation onto your jaw line, blending it gently into your skin. If it's the right color, it should "disappear," leaving behind only a smoother, more flawless finish.

PRIMING YOUR FACE

One of the keys to flawless application is to start with a clean, well-moisturized face. While cleanliness cannot be underestimated, neither can the use of a moisturizer to make the skin soft and supple and prime it for the foundation, which goes on more smoothly and adheres better when used over a moisturizer.

CREATING AN EVEN APPLICATION

Many women make the mistake of applying their foundation haphazardly, not realizing that they're creating blotchy, uneven areas on the surface of their face that appear after the foundation sets. To avoid this problem, dot the foundation sparingly on one side of the face only and begin blending by using a smooth circular motion. Then lightly pat the newly applied foundation with a slightly damp makeup sponge, working from the top of the face downward, to create a smooth even finish. The top-to-bottom patting pattern also helps lay to rest tiny facial hairs, thus helping ensure a smooth, more finished surface. Repeat the procedure on the opposite side of the face.

Special attention should be given to the hairline and jaw line, where the foundation should disappear into the skin to avoid any lines of demarcation.

Fingertips and sponges are the two most common "tools" for application, with fingertips suitable for cream foundations (sponges absorb too much cream to be efficient), sponges suitable for compact and stick foundations, and both suitable for liquid and tinted moisturizer foundations. Another option is a foundation brush using the same technique.

USING A CONCEALED WEAPON

Another important weapon in the foundation arsenal is the concealer, which is applied after the foundation to fade away under eye circles, blemishes, undesirable freckles, or birthmarks that insist on peeking through.

Concealers can be applied with the fingertips (clean, of course!), a wedge-shaped makeup sponge, or a small, slightly pointed nylon makeup brush is best for blending in without smearing (natural brushes will soak up the concealer). Proper application is easy but requires a little patience and control. The key is to apply in a gentle dabbing motion called stippling, and to continue doing so until the concealer is completely blended into the target area.

It's always best to apply a concealer after the foundation in order to avoid smearing the concealer during the foundation's application. The rules are switched when it comes to tinted moisturizers, which should be applied after the concealer.

Like foundations, concealers come in a variety of tones. To choose the one that's best for you, make sure it's half-a-shade lighter than your natural skin tone. Concealers are also available in color-correcting tones—yellow, green, and mauve. Yellow cancels out the bluish-purple tones responsible for under eye circles; green cancels out the redness found in acne scars, blemishes, and birthmarks; and mauve counteracts overly yellow skin tones.

SETTING THE FOUNDATION

Once the foundation is applied, it's time to "set" it with a light dusting of powder. To do this, use a powder puff or a compact pad to apply either a loose or pressed powder to the face by lightly pressing the powder onto the face. You can even extend the powder to the upper part of the neck.

Once the entire face has been powdered, take a large fluffy sable (or other type of natural bristle) brush that hasn't been dipped in powder and use it to blend and remove any loose or excess powder that's been left behind. To do this, you'll want to start at the forehead and brush from left to right in wide downward sweeps across the face.

For a lighter "setting" option, which may be more popular with teens and 20 year olds, forego the powder application via the powder puff and compact and simply dip a large fluffy brush in powder and apply, using the same left-to-right brushing pattern as described above. Should you decide to do this, however, it's necessary to tap the brush against your wrist once or twice after dipping to shake off any excess powder before applying.

A MORE BEAUTIFUL YOU

Once you've determined the foundation type that's right for you, chosen the most natural looking color, and applied your foundation flawlessly, you're on your way to creating one of your most beautiful faces yet. Soon others will be asking you for the secret to your beautiful, seemingly flawless face. Just tell them that . . . it all starts by building from the ground up!

FOUNDATION AND FACE COLOR TIPS

- Apply eye creams and moisturizers before foundation. The eye area especially is the first place foundation tends to crease. Mixing a few drops of shimmer lotion into liquid foundation gives a subtle gleam.

- For even coverage, apply foundation with a slightly damp sponge or foundation brush. For maximum coverage, cream covers best. For medium to sheer coverage, try liquid foundations. For maximum versatility, try wet/dry compact makeup.

- After foundation, and before powder, simulate fresh, natural flushed cheeks with a gel blush color.

- Make your own tinted moisturizer by mixing one part foundation with two parts moisturizer in the palm of your hand, then apply.

- Wear the Lamas Beauty *Overnight Treatment Tint* during the day for light makeup coverage with skin-care benefits or as a primer under foundation.

- Too red or too sallow? Correct natural skin tone under color with tinted primer. Use mint-green to neutralize redness or blotchiness. Use violet to neutralize yellow tones.

White primer will neutralize all tones to give skin a porcelain pale finish. Bronzing powder can help tone down ruddy, uneven coloring skin tones or rosacea.

- Dark olive or African American skin is often darker on the forehead where the sun hits. A slightly darker foundation might be needed in this area.

- Soak up excess foundation by pressing a clean sponge on the face, especially around the nose and mouth where foundation tends to collect.

- If foundation looks heavy at the end of the day, freshen it by dabbing a moisturizer under the eyes and smoothing it across the cheekbones. Light reflecting foundations contain particles that detract attention from lines and blemishes and add a subtle glow to mature skin.

CHAPTER THREE

Blush and Contouring
TECHNIQUES

Blusher is one of the hardest cosmetics to apply. It must be blended perfectly so there's no harsh edges and your best features are subtly enhanced. Choosing the right color for your skin tone is essential. The right color will give you a healthy glow. The wrong color will leave you looking drained or overdone. Caution: Know your best features. Emphasize beautiful cheekbones, a high forehead, or a perfect chin by using blusher to subtly highlight them.

Look at the whole picture: Always complement or match blusher to your lipstick color as well as your clothes. Cheek color should be applied after foundation or on clean bare skin, if your skin looks good without foundation. Be sure to apply a thin layer of pressed or loose power on bare skin first, then blusher, to keep oily areas from causing blush to get blotchy or streak.

BLUSH FORMULATIONS— PICK THE ONE RIGHT FOR YOU!

There are a million ways to blush out there. Go to a local cosmetic counter and try on a few formulas from your favorite brands, keeping your skin type—oily, normal, or dry—in mind. Some tips before you buy:

Powder Blush. The great all-time favorite. Perfect for any skin type. Sheer and natural looking. Convenient for touch-ups during the day. Because it's sheer, it's easy to layer using two or more colors. Many women use a beige or cocoa-brown tone to accent cheekbones and temples and slim the sides of the nose, then overlay it with a cheeky color for extra glow.

Cream Blush. A great way to blush for normal to dry skin. Cream offers more intense color than powder, so use sparingly and blend well. Especially nice for evenings under candlelight. Since cream formulas usually have the most moisturizers and/or oils, they cling better and tend to last longer on the skin. Some women use cream blush as a base, then brush a light veil of matching powder blush over it for an all-day or all-night glow.

Liquid or Gel. Beautifully lasting. Many are oil-free, which make them a better choice for oily skin than a cream blush. Some are water-resistant, too. Practice makes perfect. Start with a tiny amount on your fingertips or a sponge and build up color gradually for best results.

Cheek Pencils. Great for beginners because you have lots of control. Oily skin alert: Pencils are often formulated with extra moisturizers and emollients to keep them soft and blendable. Look for oil-free formulas. Stroke on and use your fingers to blend to a sheer veil of color.

Bronzers. Liquid, powder, gel, or cream. Instead of a rosy glow, another option is a sun-kissed look. Bronzers are ideal for faking or enhancing the golden glow of a week in Bermuda. Like liquid blush, bronzers take a little practice. Use sparingly and as directed, practicing until you get the hang of it. Bronzer is especially flattering to medium- and deep-toned complexions. Fair-skinned types should pick only the lightest shades, even if you have a tan, then blend to the sheerest hint of color.

Tinted Moisturizers. Another option for full-face glowing. Tinted moisturizers are a good 2-in-1 choice for weekends, active sports, vacations, and other times when you want just a little color plus the added bonus of moisture protection. Since there's usually more moisturizer than color in these formulas, normal to oily skin should pick an oil-free formula and use sparingly to avoid a too shiny look.

HOW TO CHOOSE YOUR COLORS

Contrary to popular belief, whatever your skin tone—fair, medium, or deep—you can blush in almost any color, but it's the intensity of color that can make or break the look. If the color is too deep or intense, it can look garish on light skins. If it's too faint, the color can disappear on medium- to deep-toned skin. If your skin has a cool cast, your best blush will probably be on the cool-toned side. If your skin has warm golden or olive tones, your best blush probably falls on the warm side.

Cool-Toned Skin. If you look best in blue, aqua, green, lavender, plum, and other cool water tones, get a rush from your blush in cool tones of plum, wine, crimson, blue-red, pastel pink, terra cotta, peach, or rose.

Warm-Toned Skin. If you look best in peach, pink, orange, red, olive-green, and other warm earth tones, get a rush from your blush in warm tones of hot pink, coral, warm red, bronze, or brown.

Blush intensity according to skin tone. Fair: light to medium intensity. Medium: medium intensity. Deep: medium to deep intensity.

HOW TO APPLY YOUR FORMULA PERFECTLY

For a sculpted, sophisticated look. First, find your cheekbones by sucking in the cheeks. Feel along the edge of the cheekbone. This is where you'll place cheek color. Never apply color above the cheekbone area. It will interfere with the eye area and actually make the skin under your eyes look puffy. Done correctly, the final effect is to make cheekbones more prominent and enhance your other features.

For a soft diffused glow. Smile to reveal the "apples" of your cheeks, which are right in the middle of the face. Apply color horizontally over this "apple" area and blend lightly. As always, keep blush at least one and one-half inches away from the nose and never brush color near the eyes.

USING YOUR FAVORITE FORMULA

Powder. Invest in a professional quality, full-bristled brush designed specifically for powder blush application. When applying powder blush, don't overload the brush with color. Excess color will only give you a harsh overdone look. Sweep brush lightly across the powder blush pan and tap gently to get rid of any excess. Stroke brush along the edge of the cheekbones in an upward motion toward the temples, without going too close to the hairline. Add a touch on the chin and another across the brow, brushing in a horizontal direction to balance the whole face.

Cream. Using your fingers, place 3 small dots on cheekbones and blend toward the temples until color is even. Blend another dot on chin to balance color.

Liquid or gel. Squeeze or stroke a dot of color on fingertip. Blend on cheekbones, working toward the temples. Reapply if needed to intensify color. Add a dot on chin and blend for balance.

Crayon. Gently make 2 to 3 light pencil strokes on the cheekbones and blend toward temples. Add a little on the chin and blend for balance.

For custom face sculpting with blush, there is an illustrated section in my book *BeautyWalk*. Your blush color can correct the contours of your face subtly, for the illusion of a more classic oval shape and a flawless bone structure. The secret is in where you place your colors to bring out some features and minimize less desirable ones.

BLUSH TIPS

- Apply lightly in sheer layers to get the amount of color you want.
- Invest in a big fluffy blush brush for a soft, even blush of color.
- Don't clash with your other colors. Coordinate blusher with lip color and your outfit.
- Don't overload your brush or apply too much color in the beginning. You'll only have to remove most of it to achieve the natural look you're after.
- Don't rub your skin hard when you blend. Blend gently with the pads of the fingers or a soft makeup sponge. Use a medium to dark beige tone for emphasizing cheekbones.
- Blend blusher inward toward the nose or downward below your cheekbone area. Always blend in an upward motion and out toward the edges of your face. Stay clear of cream blush if your skin is oily.

- In a rush? Get lip color and blush with an all-purpose 2-in-1 crayon for both.
- Apply blush after powder for smooth, even look with no streaking.
- Choose soft natural pinks, beiges, and peaches for day; go brighter at night.
- When you just want to add warmth to the skin instead of a standard blush color such as rose, peach, or plum, use a light to medium bronzing powder in place of blush.
- Simulate natural flushed cheeks with a gel cheek color.
- Look at your face from all angles after blushing to make sure every edge is completely blended.
- Wash brush frequently with soap and water. Air dry to keep it fresh.
- Wash your hands before and after you blend in cream, liquid, or gel blusher to prevent transferring bacteria to your skin and staining fingers and clothes.

CHAPTER FOUR

Creating Beautiful
EYEBROWS

B EAUTIFULLY shaped eyebrows act as a frame to set off your eyes, just as your hairstyle sets off your face and a picture frame sets off a beautiful painting. It's no exaggeration to say that brow shape can make or break your look. Well-shaped brows can also take years off your appearance. And although brow shapes may come and go, the basics of shaping stay the same.

Even if you've always been a little intimidated about how to go about brow design, here's how to create mistake-proof eyebrows every time.

SHAPING 101

1. The Basics

- Stand in front of the mirror. Look straight ahead. Try visualizing a straight line from the base of your nose to your eyebrow. (You can also use a pencil as your line, if it helps.) First, imagine the line (or place your pencil) straight up from the outside base of your nose to the brow line—ideally, that's where your eyebrow should begin (A).

- Looking straight into the mirror, imagine the line (or place the pencil) slanting across the center section of the eye to the right of the pupil. That's where the arch should be (B).

- Imagine your line (or place your pencil) angling even farther, straight past the outer corner of the

eye. That's where the end of the ideal brow line should reach (C).

2. Tweeze excess hairs, working from underneath the brow to even up and clean up the line. Does the line of the natural brow stop short of the outside corner (point C above)? No problem. Use a freshly sharpened eyebrow pencil to draw a thin delicate line to extend the brow line to the outside of the eye. Blur the color lightly with a fingertip.

3. To lift the arch of the brow higher, tweeze hairs from just below where you want the arch to be highest. This also instantly "opens" the look of the eye.

4. The eyebrows should be at their fullest at the inside edges, right above the inside corners of the eyes (A). If your eyebrows are thin or sparse, fill in with short, slanted hair-like strokes with your brow pencil. Follow with a stiff brush dipped in complementary eyebrow powder color. Use the same motion to apply it, adding more weight to the pencil color. Let the line gradually thin out as it goes past the arch of each brow (B).

SHAPING—INTENSIVE

Shaping your eyebrows beyond basic grooming is best done by a professional. Although, once you get the line and shape you want, you may be able to maintain it with regular tweezing yourself. For more extensive reshaping—with waxing, lasers, electrolysis, or threading—consult a professional and plan on regular repeat visits to maintain the look.

The best tweezers are slant-edged, with a slightly textured rough point that grasps the hair easily. You shouldn't have to yank to pull the hair. For more control, some styles come with scissor-like handles. Plan on replacing tweezers every 2 to 3 years when they get dull and lose their grip. Keep your tweezers clean.

COLOR

Always choose a brow color that matches or flatters your hair color and skin tone. In general, I prefer light, natural looking brows for day and stronger, more dramatic brows for evening. If you make a dramatic change in your hair color, lighten or darken your brows accordingly. In general, you'll find more color choices in powder brow colors than in pencils. Experiment with a few shades to find your best look. Perfectionists can even blend 2 colors together for a custom effect.

Sharpen pencils before every use for precise shaping. If you use powder formulas, wash the brush and air-dry after every 2 or 3 uses. The brush will drag, skip, and spill too much color if it's overloaded with powder.

HAIR COLOR	EYEBROW COLOR
Ashy, cool tones, brown or blond	Ashy, cool tones, light to medium brown
Red or with reddish highlights	Auburn or brownish-red
Platinum blond	Taupe, light brown, medium brown
Golden/dark blond	Medium brown or golden brown
Brunette	Dark brown or charcoal black
Black	Dark brown or charcoal black
Gray or white	Medium brown or slate gray

EYEBROW TIPS

- Start fresh. Sharpen your pencil before every application.
- Women of color can create more brow emphasis by bleaching the hair just a few shades lighter to a warm chestnut or reddish blond tone. Mix and apply a facial-hair bleaching cream and leave on the brows for a minute or two, checking to make sure you've achieved the desired lightness. If you over bleach and the effect is too light, don't

worry. You can correct with a brow powder or pencil, and you'll know to remove the bleach a little earlier next time.

- Tame wayward hairs with a tiny bit of brow fixative or Vaseline after your brow color.
- Pencils give the cleanest, most precise definition. Powders give a soft effect and need minimal blending. To heighten the arch, apply an extra bit of color at the highest peak.
- Use the Lamas Beauty *Lash Masque* to set as well as fill in eyebrows using natural coloring ingredients.
- Never draw brows downward at the ends. Strive for a winged effect.
- Pluck hairs from underneath the brow. Grasp hair at the root, pulling hair out toward the temple in a quick firm stroke.
- Pluck at night after washing your face. Dip a Q-tip in a little antiseptic or alcohol and swab over the area before and after tweezing.
- Never shave the brows.
- Never draw a new brow line above the natural one.

CHAPTER FIVE

The Art of
CUSTOM EYES

As poets have said, the eyes are the window to the soul. The right eye makeup can add to the beauty of your eyes when you know how to accent the positive and minimize any negatives.

CHOOSING YOUR EYE COLORS—
ASK YOUR CLOSET!

Colors fall into 3 categories—warm, cool, and neutral. What makeup colors look best on you is primarily determined by your skin tone and what you're wearing today. Eye and hair color come second. Your clothes closet is a great guide. If you wear warm, earth-toned colors, such as olive green, brown, terra cotta, and camel, warm tones are probably your best bets for eye color. If most of your clothes are in cool tones of blue, purple, lavender, and dark green, cool colors will look great on your eyes.

Of course, you'll never go wrong with classic neutrals—grays, ivories, taupes, and browns. These shades flatter everyone. They're also natural choices for someone whose wardrobe is all black, white, or beige.

CUSTOM EYES

For basic eye design, all you need is one eye shadow to accent, one to define, and an eyeliner pencil. For custom eye designs, I add a highlighter as an extra option plus mascara and brow pencil. To accent and define, I recommend matte powder eye colors, not frosted.

There are 3 easy steps to custom eye designs for every eye shape: lining, accenting with light shades, and defining with deep shades. The 3 tools you'll need are: 1 light-toned powder eye shadow; 1 deep-toned powder eye shadow (contrasting or complementing your light shade); and 1 eyeliner pencil—brown, charcoal, or navy. Black works best for brunettes or exotic faces. Additionally, you'll want to have: mascara, light frosted highlighter eye shadow (optional), and an eyebrow pencil that matches or is a shade darker than your own brows.

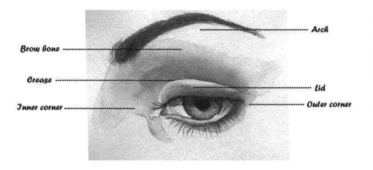

Arch

Brow Bone

Crease

Lid

Inner corner

Outer corner

THE ART OF CUSTOM EYES

First, the theory, then we practice! Know the Theory of Light, and you've mastered one of the most important aspects of makeup: *Light tones* bring features forward and out. *Dark tones* bring features in and minimize them.

Ready to practice? There are several eye shapes—even eyes, close-set eyes, wide-set eyes, deep-set eyes, prominent ("Bette Davis") eyes, round eyes, down-slanting eyes, hooded eyes, small eyes, and Asian eyes—and techniques to apply to maximize the beauty of your special eyes and minimize their limitations. In my book *BeautyWalk,* I cover all the eye shapes. For the basics here I am limiting the discussion to even eyes. Practice a few times until perfect and—I promise—you won't believe your eyes!

EVEN EYES

Even eyes are well proportioned and evenly spaced, one eye's-width apart. Your goal is to emphasize your eyes' balance and shape.

Line: Line upper and lower lid evenly. Gradually widen the line at the outer corners.

Accent: Brush light color evenly over the entire lid, lashes to brow bone.

Define: Stroke a smooth ribbon of your deep color along and slightly above the natural crease of the lid to the outer corner of each eye. Blend edges lightly.

For an extra touch: Brush a little highlighter color along the brow bone to accent. Extend the length of eyebrows or heighten the arch, if needed to maintain the balanced effect. Apply mascara evenly on top and bottom lashes.

EYE TIPS

- Lightly powder lids before eye shadow to keep it

crease-proof longer. Avoid creams that tend to crease.

- To keep eye shadow from falling under your eyes as you're applying it on the lids, apply a dusting of loose powder directly under eye area before you stroke on your eye shadow. Then, if a little shadow falls onto the skin under your eyes, it clings to the loose powder. After eye shadow is applied, whisk away any shadow fallout and the powder from under your eyes with a powder brush.

- For wider eyes and brighter whites, line the bottom rim of your eyes with a soft white eye-liner pencil.

- For fast removal, use a good eye makeup remover. It has oils that dissolve makeup better and faster than regular cleanser or toner. Then wash as usual.

- Keep pencil eyeliner from smudging by going over the line with matching powder eye shadow.

- Another way to line your eyes: Use your favorite deep-toned eye shadow, wet or dry, with an eye-liner brush.

- Keep a magnifying mirror nearby to check your work.

- Apply an eye base first if color settles into lines.

- Less is more! It's easier to build color up layer by layer than to erase too much.
- Clean up slips and smudges as you work with Q-tips moistened in eye makeup remover.

CHAPTER SIX

Lashes
101

WOMEN would rather fight than switch from their favorite mascara. But there's more to beautiful lash design than the formula—let me show you some masterstrokes.

Long sweeping lashes have been a sign of glamour and femininity since God created Eve. Using your preferred mascara, here's some quick tips to help you make the mega-lashes of your dreams in microseconds with the finesse of a pro.

CURL YOUR LASHES

Make sure your lashes are clean of old mascara and completely dry before you start.

A metal or plastic lash curler is the professional's choice. To use a lash curler, the trick is to catch all the lashes without pinching your lid. Open the scissors handle ends and press the open "mouth" of the curler gently against the upper lid, then close the handles to catch the lashes and curl them upward. Hold curler closed against lashes for at least 5 seconds to set curl. Open the scissors ends gently to release the curler. Repeat the same steps with your other eye.

If your lashes look bent instead of curled, move the curler halfway up the length of the lashes. Then squeeze and hold for another 5 seconds.

APPLY LASH COLOR

Enhance the curl you've just achieved by applying mascara right after curling. Remove brush from its vial and lightly stroke the excess off on a tissue (there's still plenty of color on the brush for lash making). Work with the upper lashes first. Look down at a slight angle into a mirror. Stroke the brush from the roots to the ends of lashes with a twirl, following the way lashes curl, up and out. Next, apply mascara on the underside of the upper lashes, brushing upward from roots to tips. Repeat until every lash is evenly coated.

For the bottom lashes, hold the mirror slightly above your face. Then hold the brush in an upright vertical position and stroke the brush from side to side, like a windshield wiper, moving from the tiny inner corner lashes to the outer lashes. Next, stroke the brush downward to smooth and coat each lash evenly with color from the roots to the ends.

For more definition, repeat application on upper and lower lashes while lashes are still wet to avoid clumps. If you get clumps, reach for a clean, dry eyelash/eyebrow comb and separate and dissolve clumps while lashes are still wet. Clean up any smudges with a Q-tip dampened with eye makeup remover.

LASH TIPS

- Curl with lash curler before mascara.
- Use the Lamas Beauty *Lash Masque* to strengthen and condition eyelashes and to increase fullness. May be worn under mascara or as an alternative to mascara and replaces the need for eyelash tinting as it contains natural coloring ingredients.
- Look for gel-based formulas and full bristly wands to coat lashes all around.
- Create more length by sweeping color, starting at

the roots to ends, in a long, smooth upward motion so color is even to the very tips. Try a lengthening formula.

- A black-brown or dark brown shade flatters most women—blondes, redheads, or brunettes. Black looks best on very dark brunettes. Plum or navy blue is also flattering on naturally dark lashes. If your lashes are light, use navy or plum as your second coat over your basic black-brown.
- Save special-effects bright mascaras for evening.
- Toss unused mascara after 3 months to avoid bacteria buildup.
- Don't apply mascara while sitting in a moving vehicle—to avoid eye injuries.
- Avoid infections. Don't share your mascara!
- Close vial tightly after use. Don't churn mascara around in the vial. It brings in more air to dry out the formula.
- Keep smudges minimal by first lightly wiping mascara wand with tissue when you remove it from the vial. Wait a few seconds between coats. And reapply as desired. Also look for a mascara wand with ridges rather than bristles.
- Most mascaras are waterproof or water-resistant these days. But for rainy days, sunning, or swimming, try a clear waterproofing topcoat.

- For more curl or to refresh curl later in day, stroke the brush to the tips of lashes and hold at an upward angle for 3 to 5 seconds.

- For an ultra-natural look, clear mascara can be used on naturally dark lashes to enhance separation and curl and add gloss without extra color.

- Lash conditioners encourage growth and silkiness. Stroke on clean dry lashes at bedtime.

- Promote lash growth through gentle handling and removing makeup every night. Use eye makeup remover with cotton balls before you wash your face to remove mascara and other eye makeup before you sleep. Gently wipe, don't scrub. In addition to being unsightly, clumps and thick coats of color can weigh fragile lashes down and encourage early breakage.

- False lashes. Even if the '60s are back, have a makeup pro trim them to match your eyes perfectly and teach you how to put them on. Professionals, by the way, usually apply fakes lash by lash, not in strips.

CHAPTER SEVEN

Great Looking LIPS

HOW TO CREATE A BASIC LIP DESIGN

HERE'S a mistake-proof way to create great looking lips anytime, anyplace, and anywhere. It's as easy as connecting the dots on a puzzle. All that is required is your favorite lipstick or lip gloss, a sharp lip pencil in the same shade or a beige neutral, and a lip brush. You can outline your lips perfectly with these simple steps:

STEP 1: With your pencil, add 2 dots—one at the edge of each corner on either side of your upper lip. Then add 2 more dots—one at each of the twin peaks (the crests) in the middle of the upper lip.

STEP 2: Connect your dots. First, connect the dot on each corner up to the dot on the crest on the same side. Then connect the 2 dots on both crests together to completely outline the top lip.

STEP 3: Outline, starting from the middle of your lower lip, lining outward three-quarters of the way to the corners, stopping right before you get to the corners.

STEP 4: Fill in with lipstick or lip gloss, using your lip brush to apply color evenly. Blend any visible edges of your pencil lines with lipstick, using your lip brush to apply and blend.

If you have thin lips, full lips, uneven lips, a small mouth, a wide mouth, or a downcast mouth, I have included steps for reshaping your lips for the symmetrical look that you want in my book *BeautyWalk*.

LIP TIPS

- For long-lasting color, try Chapstick as a lip primer, under color. The waxiness in Chapstick smoothes the lip surface, fills in tiny lines, and heals as it protects.

- Use the Lamas Beauty *Lip Enhancer* as a lip conditioning treatment for fine lines on and around the lips and to create long-lasting lip fullness. Can be worn alone (contains natural coloring ingredients) or under lipstick.

BASIC LIP DESIGN

STEP 1: With your pencil, add 2 dots

STEP 2: Connect your dots

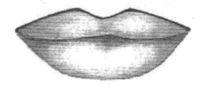

STEP 3: Outline

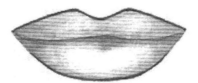

STEP 4: Fill in with lipstick or lip gloss

- You can also use a lip primer to keep lips from drying out under matte colors.
- Powder lips also gives lip color or gloss something to cling to for longer, smoother wear. Blot lips after applying lipstick to set color and remove excess. Add a thin layer of loose or pressed powder, then apply color again.
- Always blend lip liner into lips, then add lipstick or lip gloss for a sheer natural look.
- For evening special effects, apply a sheer lip gloss in silver, gold, or an iridescent shade over the lip color.
- If you have uneven amounts of natural color in your lips, neutralize your natural lip color, dot foundation on your lips, blot, then apply lipstick as usual.
- To prevent lip color "bleeding," first apply lipstick. Then dip the corner of a dry wedge sponge into loose powder and dot at the upper and lower corners of your mouth on the skin at the outside edge of the lip line. This is where "bleeding" usually occurs. Whisk away excess powder with the clean edge of your sponge.
- Create fullness with a spot of gloss in the middle of the mouth.
- Create fullness with my *Night Radiance Lip Enhancer*

Stick, which can make your lips look up to 40 percent fuller and more lush in 2 weeks or less.

- Create fullness with any basic lip primer product that smoothes out lip tissue so color goes on smoother and more reflective, giving the illusion of greater fullness.
- Create fullness by tricking the eye. The corners of your lips form a sideways V. With a liner that is one shade deeper than your lip color, line that V area on the upper and lower lips.
- Create fullness by applying gloss first. Choose a lip gloss slightly lighter than your lipstick. After you've applied lipstick, dab a touch of gloss on the center of the lower lip and blend slightly with a lip brush.
- Create fullness by highlighting. Blend a touch of concealer or highlighter at the bow of your lips and right under the lower lip.
- Turn down too much shine by holding a single-ply tissue to your lips and pressing a little loose powder through it—just enough will sift through the tissue to adhere to color and reduce the shine.
- Turn up the shine with a thin layer of clear lip gloss over lipstick or alone. For high-voltage shine and color, try a lip lacquer over lipstick or alone.

CHAPTER EIGHT

Skin-Care TIPS

ZIT FIGHTERS

- Rule #1: Don't pick! Keep your hands off your face. When you do touch your face, make sure fingers and nails are as clean as possible.
- Wash twice a day. Lightly in the a.m. Extra thoroughly in the p.m. Wash with warm—not hot—water, and lots of it. Dry face with a clean towel. If soap over dries skin, switch to cleanser or an alternate soap with cleanser, morning and night.
- Avoid washcloths. A good alternate is a disposable cleansing "facial" cloth. Use once and throw away!
- Disinfect by placing a septic stick on the zit for 30 seconds.
- To reduce redness, saturate a cotton ball with Visine and hold it on the blemish for 2 minutes or more.
- Reduce swelling or inflammation with a dab of Preparation H. Leave it on for a few minutes until

absorbed.

- Eat a healthy diet and get regular exercise to improve circulation.
- Use oil-free sunblocks or tanning lotions.
- Avoid cream-based foundation or blush if your skin is oily.
- Cut oil buildup with an oil blotting "mattifying" toner.
- Use oil-free moisturizer sparingly. A dime-sized amount is plenty.
- Exfoliate at night, once or twice a week.
- Use an acne/oily skin-fighting mask once a week.
- Have a professional facial regularly to safely extract clogged oil and dirt without infection or scarring.
- Don't over treat. Overdoing it—washing, masking, or medicating—can stimulate more oil.
- Rest on the Seventh Day. Give your skin a makeup-free day.
- See a dermatologist if acne persists.

SENSITIVE SKIN

- Use a mild unscented cleanser and warm water.
- Wash with your fingertips, not a loofa or wash-cloth.

- Use an alcohol-free toner or witch hazel or skip it completely if you find it irritates or burns.
- Avoid using strong products with Retin-A, AHAs, or glycolic acid every day. Save them for an intensive skin-care session no more than once a week. Don't overlayer these strong treatment products.
- Use PABA-free sunblock.
- Rosacea patients should avoid spicy foods, caffeine, alcohol, sun exposure, saunas, and steam baths.
- If redness or irritation persist, see your dermatologist.

NAILS AND BODY CARE

- Soothe painful hangnails by moistening first with water and then applying moisturizer or cream. Gently clip the hangnail off. A warm saltwater soak will help remove redness.
- Avoid nail color yellowing with a topcoat UV (sun) protector.
- Avoid acetone removers—they are drying and cause white spots.
- Brighten and smooth unsightly elbows with fruit acid-based moisturizers and exfoliators.
- Before bed, soak hard-callused or cracked feet (hands, too) in warm water for 3 to 5 minutes. Then spread a rich cream or alpha-hydroxy

based lotion on them until absorbed. Maximize results by wearing cotton socks or gloves over the cream or lotion all night.

- Dry itchy skin. After a warm bath, try one of the light "dry" oil sprays to direct moisturizer in hard to reach areas such as the small of the back. Avoid chlorine, harsh bubble baths, or super-hot bath or shower water until the condition improves. Use a lotion or cream everyday before you dress to keep skin soft and comfortable all day.

- Invest in a humidifier or place a pan of water on your radiator at night.

- Keep the bathroom door shut after you shower while you're applying lotion or moisturizer. Leave your towel-dried skin slightly damp and apply moisturizer to trap more water into the skin.

- Change your moisturizer seasonally—richer, heavier creams and lotions for colder months, and lighter, oil-free versions for hotter ones.

- Apply lotion or cream after waxing or shaving to avoid flakiness and itching.

- Every time your hands get wet, reach for the moisturizer to replenish.

- Use fragrance- and dye-free laundry detergent and avoid fabric softeners on clothes you wear most often. The residues can dry skin.

CHAPTER NINE

Tips on
HAIR

IN the world of beauty, hair serves much the same role as a frame—it surrounds the picture, or face, and has the potential of illuminating desirable features, downplaying less-than-desirable ones, and creating balance and symmetry. A person's face is one of the first things that a person notices about someone else. Your hair should not only frame your face but substantially transform it. Long or short, curly or straight, in any color, these tips will make it your crowning glory and the best accessory of all.

If you are looking for simple strategies to choosing the right hairstyle for the shape of your face or the right hair color, it's in my book *BeautyWalk*.

HAIR TIPS

- For a beautiful shine, slide a heated flatiron over blown-straight hair in a downward motion. The flatter the hair shaft the more it reflects light.

- The curving structure of curly hair can keep it from reflecting light as well as straight hair. Look for styling products with tiny shimmering lights or light-reflecting polymers to make your tendrils sparkle and shine. Use on wet or dry hair as directed and blow-dry, if desired.

- To increase the volume of your hair, spray on your volumizing products while hair is still damp and blow-dry as usual. Your hair will look as super lush as you want it to be without the stiff quality you get when you spray on previously dried hair. Recommended: *Lamas Botanicals Rice Protein Volumizing Shampoo.*

- Draw all eyes to your hair by wearing colors that offer the maximum contrast to your hair color. Contrast is the secret. Blondes and redheads turn heads with black, charcoal, chocolate, and navy. Brunettes draw raves with light colors, such as creams, peach, yellow, camel, and tan. Gray, salt and pepper, and white hair look sensational next to bright pinks, purples, greens, and blues.

- Dandruff is caused by an inflammatory condition that causes the scalp to be oily and flake off in tiny white flakes. Dandruff isn't caused by drying out the scalp or by blow-drying and heat styling. Eliminate flakes from your scalp and shoulders with a dandruff shampoo, 2 or 3 times a week. Recommended: *Lamas Botanicals Chinese Herb Scalp Stimulating Shampoo.* Don't use more often than that, because you risk drying out your scalp in addition to your dandruff condition. Alternate with an oily skin shampoo and light conditioner. Don't over lather, which kicks up the oil production another notch. Condition only on the ends or to permit hair to be combed tangle free. Recommended: *Lamas Botanicals Wheatgrass Deep Cleansing Shampoo with Soy Balancing Conditioner.*

- Is it dandruff or dry scalp? Your scalp is dry if it feels tight and itchy and you find fine scalp flakes in your hair. If its dandruff, your scalp may look inflamed, you notice your hair gets oily rapidly, and you find flakes not only in your hair but even in your eyebrows. Flakes tend to be bigger, too. For either condition, your best defense is a good offense. To restore a dry scalp to normal, use an extra moisturizing shampoo and conditioner plus non-alcohol styling products and hair spray. Recommended: *Lamas Botanicals Soy Hydrating Shampoo with Soy Balancing Conditioner.*

MORE HAIR TIPS

- Tone down brassiness with an ash blond or light brown rinse. Chlorine makes the problem worse.

- Frizz. There are dozens of products to fight the problem. The thicker the hair, the thicker the product you need to calm it down. In a pinch, a tiny bit of Vaseline or body lotion smoothed lightly over the top layers will settle down frizzes and split ends.

- Super straight hair. Use a hot (1600-watt) dryer. To prevent frizzing, always aim the nozzle downward and hold hair straight as you're blowing it dry.

- For smoother flowing curls, blow-dry, then follow with 10 minutes in Velcro curlers instead of hot ones.

- Heat rollers. Use the type with a steam option for firmer curls, less damage than dry heat.

- Split ends. Anti-frizz products can close up the splits temporarily, but the best way to control them is regular haircuts.

- If your conditioner weighs your hair down, condition on the ends, not the scalp.

- Cowlicks? Talk to your hairdresser about how to part, blow-dry, and cut your hair so it doesn't pop up unexpectedly.

- Use a steel brush for faster blowouts. The steel

absorbs the heat from the dryer and cuts your drying time in half.

- When your roots are showing big time and your colorist is out of town, try this: For light hair, conceal darker roots with a little foundation blended into them to cover. For dark hair, hide gray with a touch of dark brown mascara. For any color hair, pick up a color touch-up crayon in your shade to have on hand when you can't get to your colorist. They're available at beauty supply stores.

CONCLUSION

Remember, real beauty comes from within. Beauty is in the qualities of your inner soul that shine through a smile or the sparkle in your eyes and in the way you live your life. I hope that I've helped you gain an understanding of how you can look the best on the outside as well. I know it will give you a confidence that everyone finds attractive. It goes so far beyond age or trendy looks that there's no comparison!

> *"Beauty is in the eye of the beholder . . .*
> *but it is also in the eye of the possessor.*
> *What makes us truly attractive to others*
> *is the projection of our self-esteem."*
> —PETER LAMAS

PETER LAMAS is Founder of Lamas Beauty International as well as its principal product developer. Lamas Beauty International is one of the fastest growing and respected natural beauty products manufacturers in the United States. Their award-winning products are regarded as among the cleanest, purest, and most innovative in the beauty industry—products that are a synergy of *Beauty, Nature, and Science*. The company philosophy is to produce products that are safe, effective, free of harmful chemicals, environmentally friendly, and cruelty free. They insure that their products are free of animal ingredients and animal byproducts.

All of the Lamas Beauty International products can been seen and ordered from their web site, www.lamasbeauty.com. To contact them for a complete product catalog and order form or to place an order, please call toll free (888) 738-7621, Fax (713) 869-3266, or write:

LAMAS BEAUTY INTERNATIONAL
5535 Memorial Drive Ste. #F355
Houston, TX 77007

Lamas Beauty offers a full range of hair-care, body-care, and skin-care products. Some of the most recommended products include the following:

Pro-Vita C Vital Infusion Complex: Highly potent anti-aging cream that helps improve premature aging skin. Applied nightly, it defends, nourishes, and stimulates skin through a combination of three powerful antioxidants—*Vitamin C-Ester*, *Alpha Lipoic Acid*, and *DMAE* —all of which fight free radicals and help restore firm, supple, youthful-looking skin. Advanced delivery system encourages the skin's ability to regenerate, increases the skin's firmness and elasticity, minimizes the appearance of fine lines and wrinkles, and helps nurture mature skin.

Pro-Vita C Moisturizer SPF 15: Distinguished as "Product of the Year" by *Health Magazine*, as judged by dermatologists across the United States. A potent, multi-action formula to maximize protection during the day. Contains a high percentage of highly absorbable L-Ascorbic Vitamin C (one of nature's most powerful antioxidants), SPF 15 sunscreen protection against ultraviolet rays (UVA, UVB, and UVC rays), Hyaluronic Acid for intensive moisturizing, Vitamins A and E and Retinyl Palmitate (a derivative of wrinkle-smoothing Retin-A) in a unique delivery system.

Chinese Herb Stimulating Shampoo: A therapeutic special-care formula empowered with Chinese herbs used for centuries to promote healthy hair growth, stimulate and energize weak hair and scalp. Gently removes hair follicle-blocking sebum and debris that can slow growth and cause premature hair loss. This formula is mild and gentle and won't irritate, strip away color, or dehydrate hair or scalp. Helps alleviate dandruff and itchiness.

Firming & Brightening Eye Complex: Distinguished as "Product of the Year" by *DaySpa Magazine*. The major benefit of this anti-aging eye cream is its ability to lighten dark shadows and circles under the eyes through the unique natural ingredient, *Emblica*, which is extracted from the *Phyllanthus Emblica fruit* (a medicinal plant used in Ayurvedic medicine). Emblica has been shown to soften age signs, deep wrinkles, and lines as much as 68–90 percent in independent tests. Also provides intensive moisturization through Hyaluronic Acid, one of the most effective and expensive moisturizing ingredients available.

Unleash Your Greatness

AT BRONZE BOW PUBLISHING WE ARE COMMITTED

to helping you achieve your **ultimate potential**

in functional athletic strength, fitness, natural

muscular development, and all-around superb

health and youthfulness.

Our books, videos, newsletters, Web sites, and training seminars will bring you the very latest in scientifically validated information that has been carefully extracted and compiled from leading scientific, medical, health, nutritional, and fitness journals worldwide.

Our goal is to empower you! To arm you with the best possible knowledge in all facets of strength and personal development so that you can make the right choices that are appropriate for *you*.

Now, as always, **the difference between greatness and mediocrity** begins with a choice. It is said that knowledge is power. But that statement is a half truth. Knowledge is power only when it has been tested, proven, and applied to your life. At that point knowledge becomes wisdom, and in wisdom there truly is *power*. The power to help you choose wisely.

So join us as we bring you the finest in health-building information and natural strength-training strategies to help you reach your ultimate potential.